A Primer on Roman Catholicism

From his Friend

Bob Clarkle

August 15 1995

by

John H. Gerstner, Ph.D.

Soli Deo Gloria Publications
...for instruction in righteousness...

Soli Deo Gloria Publications
P.O. Box 451, Morgan, PA 15064
(412)221-1901/FAX 221-1902

*

A Primer on Roman Catholicism is © 1995 by
John H. Gerstner and Soli Deo Gloria. Some
of the material in this booklet was taken from
"The Gospel According to Rome," published
in 1948 in *The United Presbyterian* and
The Christian Union Herald.

*

ISBN 1-57358-013-9

Contents

A Primer on Roman Catholicism
by
John H. Gerstner

[EDITOR'S NOTE: This primer is intended to give an overview of the significant theological differences between historic Protestantism and historic Roman Catholicism. In a primer of this size, it is not possible to give a thorough examination of a theology that has been controverted for centuries. For a fuller treatment of the *main* difference between Catholicism and Protestantism—justification by faith alone—please see our book *Justification by Faith ALONE: Affirming the Doctrine by Which the Church and the Individual Stands or Falls* (1995)]

Recently, a Presbyterian-turned-Romanist wrote a book detailing his journey to "Rome Sweet Home." I maintain, "Rome is *Not* Home." Let me explain.

Rome affirms the Bible and its account of the creation of Adam and Eve, their temptation, and the fall of mankind by the disobedience of Adam. So Rome agrees with most Protestants that this is a fallen world and that it needs redeeming, which can only be done by God through His Son Jesus Christ. Unfortunately, the document *Evangelicals and Catholics Together: The Christian Mission in the Third Millennium* pretends that agreement on the deity of Christ and His bodily resurrection is an adequate foundation for Christian unity. As a matter of fact, there *has never been* any disagreement on those doctrines. Rome separated from the true church in the 16th century because she rejected Christ's *way of salvation!*

Let me now sketch the basic differences between Evangelicalism and Romanism. Let us begin with the lost

1

person's becoming acquainted with the way home. He gets information about a way out of his wilderness. Here Rome and Protestantism agree. Both know that a person must hear the gospel of Christ and its divinely appointed way. So Rome is involved in propagating her message, just as all Protestant churches are. Rome has a different road map from the Protestant one. Both agree, however, that unless a person gets on the Christian road he cannot find his way home to God. The views of the road may differ crucially, but there is a concurrence on the fact that the Christian road is the necessary road out of the wilderness and into God's celestial home.

From that point on, the two descriptions of the one way differ fundamentally. Both these theologies, the Roman and the Reformational, believe that lost man can grasp the meaning of salvation, of Christ, and of the atonement. When lost man does grasp the Christian message, his next step is diversely viewed by Rome and Geneva. Rome thinks that he can be persuaded of the truth of the Christian religion centering on an infallible papacy. Reformed theology believes that the Reformed pastor can prove that is not the true way, but that the Protestant, Reformational way is the biblical way.

1. BAPTISM

If the lost person is persuaded that the Roman way is the Christian way, his first duty is to be baptized. The Calvinist, however, says that once the person understands that the Christian way is the true way which he ought to accept, he neverthelesss is *incapable* of accepting it. Rome differs drastically there. She maintains that the enlightened unconverted person can see the truth of the Roman way and can decide to be baptized. The Protestant says the person can see the truth of the Reformed way and the need of baptism; but he can also see that "seeing the way" does not qualify him for baptism. According to Rome, seeing the truth of the Roman way does qualify him for baptism. According to Reformed doctrine, seeing the truth of the Reformed doctrine, including the necessity of water baptism, does not of itself alone qualify that person to be baptized.

What is the essential difference here? You see the two traditions are viewing the sinner as lost, but one of them says he is able to save himself by submitting to baptism. The other says he is *not* able to save himself by submitting to baptism. Rome says to the person, "Be baptized and you will be born again into the kingdom of God." The Calvinist says to the person, "Be baptized at this time and you will be bringing yourself under additional judgment of God by taking a sacrament you are not yet qualified to receive." Rome thinks a person even in his unregenerate state is qualified to receive baptism. Reformed Protestantism says that, in his unregenerate state, he dare not take the sign of baptism.

Do we Reformed charge Rome with heresy at this point? We certainly say she is wrong. But do we charge her with deep heresy for urging the unregenerate to be baptized in the name of the Trinity? We certainly do, because we claim that baptism is a *sign* of sin having been washed away, and that this person has not had his sin washed away because he has not yet had saving faith. Rome replies to that by saying he has not had the forgiveness of his sins as yet—that is true—but if he will receive baptism he will be born again and thus receive the forgiveness of sins by faith.

So for Rome, the baptism of an adult is not the sign of his sins having been forgiven, but the way by which his sins are to be washed away. The Reformed faith is saying, in contrast, that baptism can be administered to an adult person only if that person has professed faith and received the forgiveness of sins. Rome is saying that baptism is not a sign of the forgiveness of sins but a means to it. We are saying it is not a means to it but is only a sign when other means to salvation have occurred.

Now what are these other means of salvation to which we refer that Rome denies at this stage? The other means of salvation, and indeed the only means of salvation which we Protestants find in Holy Scripture, is the converting or regenerating work of the Spirit of God. When God has regenerated a person, and thus brought that person by the new birth into adoption into the family of God, then and only then is he to receive the baptismal sign of such membership. It is appropriate then, and only then, to be baptized. Prior to that experience, it is hypocritical for him to claim the cleansing of sins symbolically when he does not claim them actually or experientially.

Rome thinks of the candidate for baptism as an unregenerate son of the devil at the moment he receives baptism. She does not always make this clear to those whom she baptizes. But doctrinally speaking, that candidate for baptism, even though he has had a long catechumenate, is still an unregenerate child of the devil. It is that servant of Satan who is being baptized in the name of the Father, Son, and Holy Spirit at a Roman font. Such baptism does not signify that he is God's child, but assumes, in fact, that he is a child of the devil, at that point in time.

However, Rome says, the moment the water is applied in the name of the Father, Son, and Holy Spirit that person is transformed into a child of God. We admit that is *theoretically* possible. A person could be an unregenerate child of the devil and yet it could be God's plan to persuade him to come to baptism and thus become (by the Holy Spirit's regenerating work at the time of baptism) a child of God. There are Protestants who believe that as well as Roman Catholics. Why do the Reformed differ with it? We do differ with it drastically. The question right now is, what right do we have to differ with it? I will not now ask what right Rome has to teach and practice it. I rather ask the question, How can we Calvinists and Evangelicals be sure that the Roman way of bringing a person into the king-dom of God is erroneous?

There are several arguments we present to demonstrate the error of the Roman view of baptism. The first is this: If a person is a child of the devil, loves the darkness and hates the light, and hates the Christ who is the light of the world, he cannot gladly accept baptism. In truth, he wants nothing to do with the God he hates as a sinner against Him. He is a bondservant of sin. He will not go happily to something God is supposed to have established which is actually going to make him something he does not want to be.

Second, it misrepresents God's attitude toward the sinner. According to the Scripture, as even Rome admits, men are fallen and under the wrath of God. If they are not delivered, they must go eternally to suffer the torments of the damned at the hand of God. So God wants nothing to do with this person except to give him the wages of his sin, which is eternal death. But in the Roman picture of things, he is coming voluntarily and even gladly anticipating the presence of the God he hates. Meanwhile, God, who hates him with a wrath which will destroy him forever, is presumably standing there ready to convert him against his spiritual desires. That is, the sinner wants nothing to do with God. And yet here he is virtually standing and saying, "Baptize me, God, make me the kind of person who loves and serves You." That is simple hypocrisy on the part of an unregenerate sinner. Rome is playing the role of promoting hypocrisy by urging this person to come to baptism, and simultaneously suggesting that God is pleased with him even as he sinfully comes before he is regenerated.

Rome can't have it both ways. She can't say that men are fallen servants of the devil under the wrath of God who is going to punish them eternally, then at the same time say that God is well disposed to them and pleased to have them come as hypocritical sinners into His presence and receive His sacrament of baptism.

By contrast, in the Reformed view the person has been born again. He is a child of God. He is coming to Christ for the symbolic cleansing of his guilt. God has regenerated him and forgiven him and is now giving him the sign of the washing away of his sin. That is very appropriate and suitable and compatible with the doctrine of Holy Scripture and Protestantism (and even of Catholicism, if it were consistent with its view of unregenerate man).

A third indictment of Rome for this practice is that she has no ground for believing that every time baptism is administered to someone that person is born again. She does champion the doctrine of baptismal regeneration. She does teach that the sacraments "work" *ex opere operato* in their very administration.

The Bible does not teach any such doctrine. It nowhere says that everyone who is baptized is born again. It does teach that the born again should be baptized. It nowhere teaches that adults not born again should be baptized, or that, being baptized, they will be born again.

Rome tries to counter this with the contention that in Titus 3:5 baptism is represented as the washing of regeneration. "He saved us, not because of righteous things we have done, but because of His mercy. He saved us through the washing of rebirth and renewal by the Holy Spirit, whom He poured out on us generously through Jesus Christ our Savior." That text refers to the washing of rebirth or the washing of regeneration and renewal by the Holy Spirit, to be sure. It does *not* say that the washing of baptism is the washing of rebirth. Rome reads that into it. The text simply says, "He [God] saved us through the washing of rebirth and renewal by the Holy Spirit." Now the washing of rebirth and renewal by the Holy Spirit is by no means the same thing as baptism with water in the name of the Father and the Son and the Holy Spirit.

Rome will say, "Granted, it is not the same thing, but is the text not saying, when it refers to washing, that the Holy Spirit *through baptism* creates the new birth and renewal?" We say, "No, not at all." It simply says that God saves us by the washing of rebirth and renewal by the Holy Spirit. We admit that the word washing does sometimes suggest the rite of baptism. But it does not say it. Washing and baptism are not necessarily identical. It is true that baptism is a kind of washing. But every washing is not necessarily baptism. Every water baptism is not necessarily washing. The washing in Titus 3:5 is qualified by rebirth and renewal by the Holy Spirit. Even Roman Catholics admit that baptism can occur without rebirth and renewal by the Holy Spirit, and that rebirth and renewal can occur without baptism. That is the reason they say a person (be he a priest or some other person in an emergency) must have a sincere intention when he administers baptism. Presumably, if he does baptize in the triune name with a serious intention, then it "works." God regenerates. Without a sincere intention, baptism presumably does not work.

What I am observing here is that Rome admits that the baptism could occur without a sincere intention and no change would happen. As soon as you add a human factor, such as intention, you are adding something to the Titus text. Titus simply says we are saved by washing of rebirth and renewal by the Holy Spirit. It says nothing about baptism. It says nothing about intention. It says nothing about the trinitarian formula. It says nothing about water. It simply refers to the washing. It simply refers to rebirth and renewal.

Rome appeals to John 3:5: "No one can enter the kingdom of God unless he is born of water and the Spirit." This, Rome falsely teaches, is baptismal regeneration, by means of which a person is translated out of the kingdom of darkness into the kingdom of God's dear Son. But John 3:5 says this no more than does Titus 3:5. It simply says that one is born of water and the Spirit, obviously meaning born of water as well as the Spirit. John 3:3 had already said it was necessary to be born of the Spirit to enter the kingdom of God. One can be born of the Spirit. It is meaningless to say that washing with water creates a new spirit. Even those who teach the error of baptismal regeneration do not believe that. They deny any "magic" in the water. So new birth is a work of the Spirit, not of water. Why then is water mentioned in John 3:5? Obviously, baptism is associated with being born of the Spirit. It does not regenerate but is inseparable from it. How? One born of Christ professes Christ. His first confession is receiving the *sign* (baptism) of being a Christian. If he does not confess Christ he is not a Christian (Romans 10:9).

2. CONFIRMATION, OR COMMUNICANT CHURCH MEMBERSHIP

Let us now see what Rome does with a person who is deeper in the pit now than he was before he met Roman dogma and practice. She teaches seven sacraments. The first of these is baptism. Five of them have to do with the way of salvation *a la* Rome. The other two are for some members of the Roman communion, but not for all. The five salvation sacraments are baptism, confirmation, eucharist, penance, and extreme unction. The two special sacraments are ordination and matrimony. No Roman Catholic needs to be married, nor does he or she need to go into orders and become what they call "religious." But all Roman Catholics are to be baptized, to be confirmed, to receive the Mass, to observe confession and penance, and finally to have forgiveness at the time of death. We will consider only the five sacraments which deal with the way of life as they see it. Baptism has been discussed. Then comes confirmation.

Confirmation is normally administered to a baptized infant when he or she reaches 12 years of age. In the case of an unbaptized adult, it can occur any time that he is ready to profess the faith of Rome. Confirmation is based on accepting the explicit and implicit teaching of Rome.

If our criticism of baptism has been sound, the reader can see that confirmation would be a confirmation of death. It could not be a confirmation of life when no life takes place in so-called "baptismal regeneration." We have shown that baptismal regeneration is a fiction that even Rome does not hold consistently, but contradicts at various points. The point here is that if a person is not regenerated at the time of baptism, there cannot be any confirmation of an event which never took place. Rome would have administered the baptism contrary to the Lord's command, and now wrongly but consistently sees the person as ready for confirmation.

Such a "regenerate" person accepts the truth of God as represented by the Roman Catholic church. So the church instructs this person more thoroughly in the faith, which he or she affirms. As he understands more he will affirm more. Because he cannot ever understand all, he will be asked to exercise "implicit faith." Implicit faith is in the Roman Catholic teaching hierarchy. It maintains that that hierarchy, ordained and guided by God, will teach the truth of God. Though the person does not know all that the church has taught in the past, not to mention all that she may teach in the future, he simply accepts the church as appointed by God to be the infallible interpreter of truth. Therefore, whatever she says, he will believe.

That is in and of itself a very consistent view. If Rome did have the role which she claims, I too would place implicit faith in everything she teaches.

We Protestants ascribe ultimate authority to the Word of God while Roman Catholic parishioners ascribe that to the Roman church. That is, we believe that the Bible is the Word of God. We acknowledge that we have never begun to know all the teachings of the Bible. We do know that anything it does teach is true. We do not have to hear what it is before we accept it. We accept it because of its source. Its authority is its being the Word of God. God cannot err. Therefore His Word cannot err. Therefore anything it teaches is true. Whether we at the present moment know what it teaches in a given area or not, we know this: What it teaches in a given area is true. We also know that the moment we know what it teaches in that area, we know the truth in that area. We are full of implicit faith. I, for one, know that I have far more implicit faith than explicit faith. That is, I know far less about the teachings of the Bible than I am ignorant of the teachings of the Bible. Though over 80 years of age, I am far, far from ever exhausting all the truths and have only minimal knowledge. But I do know that whatever you discover and can show me is the teaching of the Bible, that is not only your truth but it is my truth.

We have Protestant debates, but the debates are simply as to whether we are correctly interpreting the Bible or not. We do not debate about the truthfulness of what the Bible says. We may debate one another as to whether he or she correctly understands the Bible. Debate ends the moment we have become persuaded of the Bible's teaching. We have implicit faith in everything it teaches from today to eternity.

Rome claims all that for her magisterium, the hierarchical church. Excuse me for laughing. This is an awful comedown from the Protestant parallel to it. It is one thing to believe that God cannot err. It is another thing to believe that the Pope cannot err when he speaks *ex cathedra*. But that is what all Romanists have to believe. The hierarchy cannot err. Whatever a synod of the church has ever ascertained (the Pope assenting or confirming or agreeing or really establishing it), that is the truth of God. If you do not believe that, you cannot be confirmed as a Roman Catholic. If you do believe that, I am sorry to say, you confirm yourself as an unbeliever. You cannot believe in God and believe that any present human beings have the authority of God. But that is what you have to believe if you want to be confirmed as a Roman Catholic!

Let me remind the reader that confirmation rests on the parishioner's accepting all that the Roman church teaches, including her fatally wrong doctrine of justification.

In the 400-plus-year controversy on justification, it is usually said that Rome teaches justification by works and Protestantism justification by faith. That description is true and false. It is true and false depending entirely on whether one understands the meaning of justification by works in Romanism and the meaning of justification by faith in Protestantism. (See section 7 of this primer.)

Most of the persons who comment on justification do not understand either the Roman view of justification by works or the Protestant view of justification by faith. So on the "article by which the church stands or falls," there is a singular, widespread, almost omnipresent misunderstanding. Persons engaged in the Reformation debate usually did understand the issue. John Calvin certainly understood it, though he used some rather imprecise language at times. Cardinal Bellarmine understood it as a defender of the Roman doctrine. But that cannot be said of all the Roman theologians at the Council of Trent (1546–63).

Speaking generally about Trent, I would say that while it correctly stated some parts of the doctrine, comprehensively speaking, it did not articulate soundly the doctrine which it anathematized. If that is so, it means that after the Reformation had maintained clearly the central doctrine at issue, the Roman church rejected the Protestant position without fully understanding or articulating it. If that is so, it is sad indeed.

It is impossible to overestimate the importance of understanding this extremely critical doctrine. If many of those who waged war concerning it did not know whereof they spoke and thought, that is a warning to all who come today to consider this crucial teaching.

If one understands the way the proponents advocated these positions, he can accurately say that Rome teaches justification by works and Protestantism teaches justification by faith alone. According to the Council of Trent's "infallible" definition of justification, the "root" of it is faith. This faith, informed by love, produces good deeds as its fruit. When a perfect measure of good works is achieved, the person enters heaven. "Saints" actually inherit the kingdom of God or go to paradise as soon as they die. Those Romanists who have not achieved that degree of perfection in this world must suffer further punishment for their remaining sins in purgatory. When they have suffered sufficiently, they will, by the merit of the works which they did, go to heaven. That is justification *by* works, *on the basis of* works, on the *merit* of works (even though Rome formally attributes all "merit" to Christ). In that sense, the Roman Catholic church teaches that justification before God is an achievement of the human being who does the works of righteousness perfectly.

This teaching of Rome is misunderstood and virtually caricatured when it is represented as teaching justification by works *alone*. According to Rome, faith is the "root" of these works. One cannot do works pleasing to God apart from faith in Jesus Christ. No wonder many Roman Catholics become enraged with Protestants who accuse them of teaching justification by works apart from any faith whatever.

Romanists believe that faith is essential, just as Protestants believe that faith is essential. They do not think it is *sufficient* for justification, but they do not believe justification can come about *apart from faith.*

It is true that Rome teaches that ultimate justification is by the works or good activities of the baptized person. They will accept that attribution. They think it is true and infallibly defined by the Holy See itself. But do not tell a Roman Catholic that he is opposed to faith or does not believe in faith or does not realize the necessity of faith. He does indeed. The Council of Trent stressed the fact that faith is necessary as the root of the good works which we do for justification. *Roman Catholicism teaches justification by works alone, but not by the works that are alone.*

The reader can see that I am playing with the Reformation formula. The Reformation insisted that *justification is by faith alone, but not by the faith that is alone.* Justifying faith is working faith. Faith produces good works. Those works do not contribute to the justification, but they are inseparable from the faith which does justify. Likewise, Rome is saying, "Justification is by works alone, indeed, but not by the works that are alone. Works are dependent on faith. Faith leads to the works. So yes, we Romanists believe in justification by works alone, but not by works that are alone."

Now that we are seeing the two positions properly and comparing them properly, let us evaluate the Roman position and, later, the Protestant position. Understanding Rome to teach justification by works in the manner just explained, is that doctrine the sound, biblical, saving doctrine of justification? Rome says it is. What does the Protestant say? As we know, Protestants in general, and the Reformed in particular, say it is not the true doctrine. It is not the saving justification of Holy Scripture.

So the question before us now is why do Protestants say that, and can such a contention be proven? We prove it this way. First, after a person is regenerated, he is still not fully sanctified. His corrupt nature is crucified and dying, but it is not yet dead. That is the reason Scripture is urging the saint to put to death the old man, and to clothe himself with the new man, to put away the works of darkness and to put on the works of light. The Lord's Prayer teaches us to confess our sins. As long as a man is required to confess his sins, he must have sins to confess.

Rome seems to feel that her "religious" are like that servant who did not only what he was required to do in the field, but did what he didn't need to do—serving his master in his spare time at home (Luke 17:7ff). But there are no works of supererogation. Every man and woman is required to be perfect as the Father in heaven is perfect (Matthew 5:48). They are to serve God with all their heart, soul, mind, and strength, loving Him and their neighbor as themselves. That is minimal duty for every person. If, therefore, a man is *able* to serve the Lord in a ministry by being celibate, he has the *obligation* to serve the Lord in that ministry by being celibate. It is perfectly true that marriage is legitimate for any man or woman, but not true for that man or woman who thinks that he or she can serve God more fully in the celibate state. If that person has the gift to live the celibate life, he or she has the duty to do so. Such persons are not going beyond

the standard of perfection, they are only conforming to
it.

Our Lord indicates that not everyone has that gift
(Matthew 19:11–12). Those who do not have the gift for
living a continent, celibate life have no obligation to avoid
marriage. On the contrary, it is better to marry than to
burn (1 Corinthians 7:9). Perfection is the standard and
the goal for every person. If a person has "celibacility,"
and concludes that they can love God with all their heart,
soul, mind, and strength, and love their neighbor as
themselves better as a celibate than as a married person,
they have no option to marry. Rome sins in making
something mandatory for religious orders which God
does not make mandatory. God does require every person
to serve God perfectly, and to do so by the celibate life if
and only if he has the gift to live continently in such a
condition. Rome requires everyone who would be an ordained minister of the Word to forego marriage, whether
he has the gift or not. The history of the church is full of
the lapses from that model and terrible sins which men
and women have brought upon themselves and others by
endeavoring to do something they had no gift from God
to do, but only a command from the church, counter-
manding God, which Rome is wont to do.

The Roman church's salvation does not begin where
she says it does, with baptism. Nor can it continue, as she
says it does, in sanctification. And if there were sanctification, it would achieve no merit, which she claims. Certainly, if there were any merit in it, the most meritorious of all
individuals is told by Scripture to say, "I am an unprofitable servant," Luke 17:10 Unprofitable servants do not
aspire to heaven on the basis of their perfection.

So Rome has not begun on the way, and even if she

had she has not continued on that way. Her way to heaven is merit, and the Bible makes it perfectly plain that no mere human ever achieved justification by his merit. Our duty here is perfection. By divine grace it will be achieved in heaven. It will not be achieved in this world even by the truly regenerate, though they must ever strive for it.

So we see that the Roman Catholic way of justification is not the way of justification but of damnation. Why do I say damnation? Is the implication not obvious? If justification is the way by which a person is made just and acceptable to God, and the person is not justified, does he not remain in the state of condemnation from which justification alone could deliver him? That is to say, if Rome does not achieve justification, as I have shown she could not possibly do on her principles, she leaves the person in the state of condemnation in which he was born. Only now there is an aggravated guilt. Rome gives him the impression, falsely, that he is no longer in a state of condemnation, but actually is in a way of salvation. His last condition is far worse than his first when he entered the Roman church, by which he is made twofold more a child of hell (Matthew 23:15).

So the author of the book *Rome Sweet Home* denies the only way of justification, and yet fancies, by false Roman doctrine, that he is on his way to justification. *If he really understands and believes the Roman Catholic way of salvation, he is in a state of condemnation worse than the one when he first believed this false gospel!* How I pray that he and his followers may see that his last condition is worse than his first, and seek the Lord, who alone justifies, while He may be found.

Rome teaches different methods of sanctification. She

believes in prayer, for example. One would be inclined to say that anyone who prays would surely be blessed by a prayer-hearing and a prayer-answering God. So whatever other error she may have in her scheme of salvation, certainly calling upon her people to pray regularly the Lord's Prayer and other prayers, and leading them in prayer in worship services and so on, is an unmitigated good. However false their system may be, certainly this is a redeeming element: prayer.

But is it? Scripture says that the prayer of the wicked is an abomination to the Lord (Proverbs 15:9; 21:27; 28:9). Prayers like that would be better unmade. God is alienated by such rather than cultivated. He is angered rather than inclined to bless. Someone might say, "But look, He is a prayer-hearing and a prayer-answering God." Yes, He is, but He is not an abomination-hearing God. The prayer of the wicked is not a prayer, it is an abomination. The way we would write that particular proverb would be by putting prayer in quotes, and reading it like this—"prayer" is an abomination. It is not prayer, it is a parody of prayer; it is a takeoff on prayer, a counterfeit of prayer, a mockery of prayer. An abomination is better left unuttered. Peter tells us that is the way pagans live who choose "living in debauchery, lust, drunkenness, orgies, carousing and detestable idolatry" (1 Peter 4:3). The prophecy of Amos has a section in which he represents wicked, unbelieving people offering sacrifices and singing and praying to God. God's response is to cover His eyes, stop His ears, and hold His nose as the incense ascends. That incense is putrid when offered by the wicked. The hypocrites make worship into a crime against the Most High. He will by no means clear the guilty of such "prayer."

The indictment of prayer in the Roman system may be the hardest one for the reader to bear. But you can see that once a person starts on the wrong road, then everything he does on that road is going to bring him closer to final destruction. Rome has started on the wrong road, and even if she does some things which are externally right, she still is on the wrong road and is moving closer all the while to destruction. People must recognize and remember this fact; otherwise they will be easily deceived into thinking that they are on the right road because they are doing some right things along the wrong road.

I call these "bad good works." I mean by that that they are bad in their motivation because the person is wrongly related to God in the first place, even though the things themselves, such as giving money in church or kneeling to pray or going the second mile with someone who has misused you, are good in themselves. They are corrupted by the source from which they come. They are, as we say, poisoned springs. Even good things are poisoned when they come from a poisonous source. Mafia members often pray about their "hits."

Manifestly, if one confuses this matter, he is prone to think he is an acceptable individual because a particular thing he is doing is in itself acceptable. As long as he is an unacceptable person, all that he does is unacceptable.

As a matter of fact, it becomes more offensive than ordinary evil deeds. An evil *person* always does evil deeds, even though they may appear to be good—grapes among thorns. When one seems to be doing what is good, and purports to be doing what is good, and claims to be doing what is good, and is considered by people as doing what is good, he is playing the role of hypocrite in all these circumstances. Hypocrisy makes a seeming good work worse

than an obviously bad work for the simple reason that it
seems to be what it is not. Evil as evil is at least seen as what
it really is. Evil seen as good is a compounded evil. So
none can sin like the saint. That is, none can sin like a
person who seems to be a saint while actually being a sinner in false clothes. He is a wolf in sheep's clothing. None
can blaspheme like the pious. "As it is written, 'God's
name is blasphemed among the Gentiles because of you' "
Romans 2:24. You are a devil appearing as an angel of
light. And the devil is never more devilish than when he
appears as an angel of light.

I will not go on with this theme any longer because it
ought to be apparent to everyone. But let me mention
just one other matter before I proceed. Take the matter of
a Roman Catholic observing the Lord's Supper, which
they call the Mass. Let's right now overlook the fact that
the Roman church wrongly deprives the people of the
cup of communion, restricting that to the clergy. Also let
us overlook the error of their doctrine of transubstantiation. That is, let us overlook any faults there may be in
communion as administered by the Roman Catholic
church. Let us simply consider it as an act of purported
obedience to Christ who commands us to observe the
Lord's Supper until He comes again. Is it not clear that
even when a group of falsely professed Christian people
profess to do this communion in remembrance of Him
they are sinning most profoundly? Yes, the communion is
commanded by Christ. Yes, it is a duty of Christian people. Yes, it is a moment of greatest fellowship with God if
it is done properly. But it is not right if the participant is
himself not reconciled to God. If we have correctly shown
that the Roman way of reconciliation is non-reconciling
and actually alienates more than does making no such

profession at all, then manifestly this person has no right
to come to the Lord's Supper at all. So while it is a duty of
true Christian people to come, it is a duty of unconverted
persons not to come, unless they choose to eat and drink
damnation, as Paul says.

→ You shrink from this, but the conclusion is inevitable
that when an unreconciled Roman Catholic comes to the
Lord's table, he eats damnation. At this particular point,
you cannot help but observe rather sardonically that the
Roman error of depriving the people of the cup turns
out to be a benefit to her people, preventing them there-
by from drinking condemnation and confining them
solely to eating condemnation. The priest, of course, by
participating in both the bread and the cup, brings upon
himself a double condemnation.

So that which virtually every Catholic considers a high
point in his journey toward heaven, namely communion,
is where he touches spiritual bottom. There is no place at
which a person can be more sacrilegious than when he
eats and drinks condemnation to himself by participating
in a communion to which he has no right.

✳ 3. THE MASS

Let us now consider the Roman Catholic eucharist in
itself. I have been considering sacraments as received by a
person who is not qualified to receive. Now let us look at
the doctrine itself as Rome promulgates it before the
world. It is not only that it may be abused by people who
use it unqualifiedly. What I will now show is that it is in-
trinisically and in itself, as understood and taught by the
Roman church, a travesty of that which the Lord Himself established.

Everyone knows that the Roman church teaches transubstantiation. Virtually everyone knows what that means. Somehow the bread becomes the body of Christ. The substance of the bread is changed into the substance of the body of Christ. The result is that when a person communes properly he actually eats the body of Jesus Christ miraculously present now in the transubstantiated bread. When the priest drinks the cup, he drinks the very blood of Jesus Christ now miraculously, corporeally, and substantially present in the cup.

I will ignore here the contention of Rome that the person does not taste what tastes like flesh, and he does not drink what tastes like blood, because of the nature of "substance." The teaching is that it is the "accidents" of anything which a person actually encounters in an experience with it and not the "substance." So a person actually devours the substance of the body of Christ. Because it is the substance and not the accidents of His body, it does not taste as if the person were actually masticating the body of Christ and drinking the blood of Christ. It is a fact even though it does not seem to be a fact. It is a fact because it is a transubstantiation of the substance but not a transubstantiation of the accidents of the substance.

This is just by way of reminding the reader what the doctrine is. My concern here is to show that there is no biblical warrant for such teaching. The first thing we observe is that to say Christ's body is literally present in the bread is a meaningless proposition. When we were considering baptism, we noticed that even though Jesus says (John 3:5) that we cannot enter the kingdom of God except by *water* and the Spirit, we know that He does not mean, and could not mean, that the water itself has the power to convert. There is no magic in the water, nor does God use it miraculously. While Christ is making it very clear that baptism is necessary, it is also obvious that it is not necessary as being power-water when actually all the power is in God.

Here too we have a situation like baptism. One cannot entertain a conception of bread being *literally* the body of anyone, not to mention the body of Jesus Christ. Bread is bread and it cannot be something other than that as long as it remains bread. Roman Catholics will say I am being rationalistic here. They will say that I am not being truly humble, accepting the teaching of the Bible which has Jesus saying, "You must eat My flesh," and "This is My body which is given for you," in the Lord's Supper. "That is what the Lord says and, whether you can understand it or not, you'd better believe it!"

I am not trying to be wiser than God, nor do I have the colossal audacity to reject His teaching and substitute my own. What I am saying, as a child of God trying to grasp the words of God, is that there is no meaning for the human intellect in saying that bread is the body of Jesus Christ. The resurrected body of Jesus Christ is at the right hand of God the Father in heaven right now, and will remain there until He comes again in His body to "judge the quick and the dead." He is not in this piece of bread, nor is His blood in the cup we drink.

When we contradict the Roman Catholic testimony of people (in their great exuberation and jubilation when they receive the wafer in their mouth), we are not denying their *experience*. They usually reply to our criticism by accusing us of consummate arrogance. They say, "You claim to know that we do not have an experience which we say we have? Aren't you being very, very presumptuous? How can *you* know what we do experience or what we do not experience? How are you qualified to say we do not actually have this immense transforming satisfaction in participating in the Mass?"

I am not denying anybody's experience. As long as I believe as I do, that they are honest persons, I am sure that they are testifying to feelings which they truly have. Nor do I deny that they are having those feelings when they are actually eating that wafer which the priest puts on their tongue. Nor do I deny that when they eat that wafer they think they are devouring the body of Jesus Christ. Nor do I question them when they say that "we have this experience because we are eating the very body of our Savior who died to save us." I do not doubt that they *think* that is the case. But I do not only doubt, but I am certain that is not the case, and that I can prove it.

You see, there are two points at issue, not only one. These people are saying two things: (1) we have this wonderful experience; and (2) this experience comes from our masticating the body of Jesus Christ. Now I am not questioning that they have this experience. I am not questioning, in other words, the first part of their affirmation. What I am questioning is the second part of their statement, that this experience comes from the masticating of the body of Jesus Christ. They believe that as firmly as they testify to the experience they have based on that belief. But the *experience* is one thing, the *basis* for it is another. The experience can be theirs, without doubt. But the masticating of the body of Jesus Christ, which they think is the source of it, is utterly impossible, I say.

There is nothing arrogant about making that statement. I am not presuming even to know their feelings except as they reveal them to me. But is it any presumption for me to question whether they can have ever masticated the body of Jesus Christ? If I can show that they could not have, that it is *impossible* to have, masticated the body of Jesus Christ in the Mass, then have I not demonstrated the second part of their testimony is absolutely false, even though they *believe* it to be true, and feel joyful for so believing?

I do not have to do this because I have already shown that there is no warrant for believing in transubstantiation. It is not taught by the Bible, nor is it even rational to the human mind. A finite body can only be in one place at one time. It is a doctrine of Roman Catholic orthodoxy as well as Protestant orthodoxy that the body of Jesus Christ is a finite body. It is also a part of Roman orthodoxy as well as ours that Christ is corporeally present at the right hand of God in heaven right now. So if a finite body has to be at one place at one time, and the body of Jesus Christ is in heaven now and not on earth, then it follows immediately that His body is not on earth anywhere. Christ's body is not in the wafer nor any place else, not to mention on thousands of different altars. Christ's body is only in heaven.

If we have proven that, we have proven those to be false witnesses who claim that their exhilaration at eating the wafer comes from actually masticating the body of Christ. That is impossible. The body of Jesus Christ is in heaven. You cannot see it or touch it, much less eat it. Your experience may be real, but the basis on which you rest it is nonexistent. It is nonreal.

I do not presume to say where these people get their feelings, but I do presume to say as a sane human being, along with the rest of the human race, that there is no way of conceiving that the body of Jesus Christ is in that wafer that Romanists eat at the Mass. I beg Romanists to realize that, though they may have a wonderful feeling, it does not come from the so-called sacrifice of the Mass.

If it cannot possibly come from that source, and if they realize that, then they can ask themselves, "How do I come to feel so exhilarated and joyous when I participate in the Mass?" They will know the nonanswer is that they have masticated the body of Christ. It is *not* that, whatever else it may be. An intelligent person will realize that if it is not what he *thinks* it is, he will become extremely dubious about the experience based on it. It is based on he knows not what, because what he thought it was based on it could not possibly be based on.

It is a sad fact that people can have exhilarated feelings about something they believe which is later demonstrated to be nonexistent. People hear at times that they are inheriting fortunes, and of course they are delighted at the prospect of having so much cash suddenly. As soon as they realize that was a false report and they do not have the cash, then exhilaration collapses and they wish they never had had it. This is what I think would happen to any Roman Catholic who sits down and deliberately thinks through this matter. It ought to lead to his conversion to realize that all his joy is resting on a non existent fact, and that he is involved in perpetuating a fundamental fraud to the whole world, namely, that he is happy because of an experience which he could not possibly have had.

Romanists (and some Protestants) will charge me with rationalism for denying that a body can be at many different places at the same time. I am being rational (as the Bible is), not rationalistic. Christ has *one* body, not many bodies as transubstantionism affirms. Every Sunday, He is supposed to have different bodies all around the world.

That would not be a thousand miracles, it would be a thousand lies. Christ miraculously *multiplied* one boy's lunch. He does not *multiply* His one body. The very utterance of such an absurd error involves a half-dozen Christological and hermeneutical errors.

4. PENANCE

Another one of the seven sacraments of the Roman Catholic church which we want to look at briefly is the penitential system. This system begins with a contradiction in terms. The Roman church teaches that when a person is born again and repents, he is forgiven. The guilt of his original sin is canceled. The remaining sin (which Rome calls concupiscence) is not sin at all. I say this is a contradiction at the very beginning of the penitential system. It says the sin has been forgiven and is no longer sin but is now concupiscence. Nevertheless, it has to be repented of and it has to be punished.

The nonsensical character of this teaching may be seen more evidently by contrasting it with the understandable Protestant view. Even a person who may not believe the Protestant view will see that it is comprehensible, while the Roman view, even if he does believe it, is not comprehensible. So I am requesting all of you, whether you are Protestant or Roman or secularist, to read carefully as I try to show that the Roman view is actually a contradiction in terms. That is to say, the Roman church teaches that original sin is really remitted and the remaining sin is not sin at all, but they treat it as if it were. Manifestly, as soon as you treat something as if it existed when, according to your teaching, it does not exist, you are communicating incomprehensibles. It would have to be one or the

other. Either it is sin or it is not sin. Either it is punishable
or it is not punishable. You cannot have something which
is sin and yet not sin, punishable and yet not punishable.
Yet this is the heart of the penitential system which in
many ways is the heart of the Roman Catholic lifestyle.

To make matters more absurd still, the punishment of
non-sin actually continues into purgatory. Persons who
go to purgatory are persons whose sins in this world have
not been adequately punished in this world. We have already indicated that, according to Roman theory, these
things are being punished in this world, not to mention
punished further in the world to come, are not sins at all!
But that is the oxymoronic Roman Catholic penitential
system. The penitential system which is what is occupying
most Roman Catholic minds most of the time is, strictly
speaking, a nonexistent system, an incomprehensible system.

Someone is very inclined to say at this juncture,
"Gerstner, you are the one who is talking in contradictory
terms. You are telling millions of people who are living in
this system that they are living in a nonsystem. Now who
is the idiot around here, they or you? Aren't you like a
person saying to a flesh-eating animal that flesh-eating
animals cannot eat flesh?" Yes, if you wish to put it that
way. This doctrine is as absurd as saying that a certain
creature is a flesh-eating animal who cannot eat flesh.
Man is a person who has no sins, but whose sins must
nevertheless be punished in this world and in the world
to come. When you ask how I can be sane when I contradict something that millions of people testify to, my answer ought to be very evident. Crazy as it may sound,
they are testifying to something which does not and cannot exist. They must have some sort of coherent concept

in their own minds if penitence is meaningful to them. What they must have in their own minds which is meaningful is, however, not what the Roman Catholic church teaches which is unmeaningful, nonmeaningful, impossible to be understood meaningfully.

I will now point out the Protestant way to show the absurdity of the Roman view in contrast to a comprehensible view. Protestantism, I would say, is a meaningful teaching, that a person can understand who nevertheless may deplore it, hate it, and reject it. But he can know what it is. Even though he rejects it, he knows what he is rejecting. If he accepts it, he knows what he is accepting. The Roman view, by contrast, is something which a person cannot know, whether he says he believes or disbelieves it.

The Protestant doctrine teaches that all the *guilt* of a person's sin (past, present, and future) is eternally forgiven the moment he receives justification by the imputation of Christ's perfect righteousness. Also, the *power* of his remaining sinfulness and sins remains but does not reign. These remaining sins bring chastening (not wrath or punishment), by his Father who loves him and for that reason chastens him so he becomes more and more like the One who died for him. That is understandable doctrine, and the Bible proves it true.

5. LAST RITES

This last of the five common sacraments requires only brief comment. It represents no new principle. It is only the final transition before death to the next world of purgatory or paradise. Since Vatican II, it is not restricted to "Last Rites" (extreme unction), but is more commonly related to anointing for serious sickness.

These sacraments and theological principles which I refer to briefly here are more fully treated elsewhere in the book *Justification by Faith ALONE,* published by Soli Deo Gloria in 1995. I append this discussion only to show how far *away from* home these sacraments and principles will carry all who sincerely adopt them.

I don't fear the Roman theologians who will simply reject what I have written. All they can do is reject, not refute. For slaves of men that is all that is necessary, alas! The next event on the divine calendar, however, is to appear before the Judgment Seat of the Lord Jesus Christ (2 Corinthians 5:10).

The ones I do fear (because they are so pervasive, though even less persuasive) are those who raise the banner of freedom of religion. They take the *legal* right to believe whatever one pleases to be a *moral* right. Our government allows all sorts of hell-deserving religions to flourish and carry millions with them to perdition. These "religious" people hate argument, detest debate, and refuse even to listen to friends who would save them from ruin. They consider it a crime even to try to prove error and save souls.

But to all who are seeking "Home," I dedicate this essay, hoping that they may come to realize and believe that only the way of the cross leads home. Perhaps the best way to show these people the true way to true *home* is to point them again to the only divinely inspired map, *Holy Scripture.*

6. THE BIBLE

There are two fundamental points at which Rome deviates concerning the Bible on the Bible's view of itself:

First, Rome denies that the Bible is a self-interpreting revelation. The Bible declares itself to be self-explanatory. This is called the doctrine of the perspicuity of the Scriptures (the see-through-ableness of the Scripture). It may be understood in its own light. What is obscure in one passage will be clearer in another. What is incomplete here is completed there. What is a figure in one place is a commentary in another.

Rome has substituted for the doctrine of the perspicuity of the Scriptures the doctrine of the audacity of the Church. The Bible says that those who run may read; Rome says that those who run to *her* may read. The Bible says of the Bereans who searched the Scriptures that they were noble; Rome says of the Reformers who searched the Scriptures that they were heretics. The Scriptures say, "Study to show thyself approved unto God, a workman that needeth not to be ashamed, rightly dividing the word of truth," 2 Timothy 2:15. Rome says, "Study to show thyself a slave obediently accepting the word of Rome."

"But," the Roman Catholic church maintains, "the Word of God needs an interpreter."

"If so," replies the Protestant church, "the word of the pope also requires an interpreter." If the Bible must be interpreted by the Church in order to render its meaning certain, then the interpretation of the Church will have to be interpreted by another authority to make its meaning certain, and then there will need to be an interpreter of the interpreter, and so on *ad infinitum.*

Now if the Romanist replies, "Where there are divergent views on the Bible teaching there must be some authoritative decision," we will agree. Nor do we only agree. Our various Protestant church courts actually provide authoritative interpretations on most points when such decisions are necessary. But there is a difference between authoritative and infallible decisions. Compare, for example, the necessity for an authoritative interpretation of the Constitution. A Supreme Court performs that task. Yet what American believes the Supreme Court is infallible? Still, its decisions prevail as a matter of necessity. On occasions the Court may be "stacked" and its interpretations biased. In the long run, however, the people of this land believe an authoritative interpreter necessary, but never do they regard it as infallible. The Constitution remains the law of the land, not the Supreme Court. Likewise, the Bible remains the law of the Christian, not the Church.

The Roman Catholic church proclaims itself to be "the pillar and ground of the truth," since 1 Timothy 3:15 says that the church is the pillar and ground of the truth. But that verse does *not* say that the Roman Catholic church is the pillar and ground of the truth; in fact, the Roman Catholic church did not even exist when this verse was penned. Additionally, where did the Church get the idea that it is the pillar and ground of the truth? From the Bible! It is the Bible which is the basis of the church's authority, not the church which is the basis for the Bible's authority. The Bible is the pillar on which the church rests; the church is not the pillar on which the Bible rests. Incidentally, the expression that the church is the pillar and ground of the truth does not point to a pillar on which truth rests, but to a pillar on which truth was posted for public announcement in antiquity. In other words, it refers to the church as witness to the truth and not the basis of it.

The Protestant church has provided for authority so that decisions can be rendered when necessary, but has avoided the error of investing this authority with infallibility. The Protestant church, not being infallible, can err, has erred, will err. There is one error, however, which it has not made and that is the greatest of them all—the error of thinking it cannot err.

Having considered Rome's first great denial, namely, that the Scripture is self-interpreting, we will consider her second great denial: that the Scripture is a complete revelation.

"Wherein is the Scripture incomplete?" we ask. No infallible answer has been given to that question, but there are a dozen or more doctrines which the majority of Roman theologians agree are only imperfectly revealed in the Bible, or merely implied, or entirely omitted.

Let us examine one of each of these classes. The Trinity, for example, Rome regards as imperfectly revealed in the Scripture. What, then, has the Church added? That God is one as to substance and three as to person. We agree. But still our philosophical interpretation of the simple Bible teaching may turn out to be quite wrong. And besides, the important thing is *that* God is one God and yet three persons, not *how* He thus exists. Yes, something new has been added (that the substance and personality of God are distinguishable) but it may be wrong. Furthermore, the explanation is not necessary to a knowledge of the Trinity. And finally, what is necessary and certain is already contained in the Bible.

Note as an example of the second group, doctrines merely implied, infant baptism. Church practice sanctions this rite. Well and good. But how did the Church come to sanction it? Undoubtedly because the Church believed that infant baptism was clearly implied in the Scripture! So the very Church tradition that is supposed to add force to the Bible rests on the Bible and has no more validity than the biblical implication.

Note finally as an example of the third class, doctrines entirely omitted in the Bible, purgatory. Here Rome is creating her doctrine out of whole cloth. Purgatory is not only omitted by the Bible, it is utterly precluded by the constant biblical teaching of two and only two possible destinies which face every man.

In order to harmonize such doctrines as purgatory, the immaculate conception of Mary, the infallibility of the pope's official declarations, etc., Rome is obliged to wrest the Scriptures. She is no more able to serve the two masters, tradition and the Scriptures, than were the Pharisees. She has had to cleave to one and abhor the other. Unfortunately, it has been the word of man rather than the Word of God which has been the preferred master.

This reminds me of the art collector who had a painting of the Leaning Tower of Pisa in his office. Each morning when he came in he would notice that the painting was hanging askew. Finally, his bewilderment drove him to ask the maid if she knew how it happened that every morning the painting was askew. She had a ready explanation: "I have to fix it that way in order to make the tower hang straight." Rome, likewise, is obliged to wrest the Scriptures in order to allow her tradition to hang straight.

7. JUSTIFICATION BY FAITH ALONE

Martin Luther, the great reformer, while still a Roman Catholic, had an experience which was the cue to his whole career. It occurred, according to his son, Paul, when, mounting the holy staircase of Rome on his knees in penance, he realized in a sudden flash of understanding the meaning of these words: "The just shall live by faith," Romans 1:17. Immediately he rose from his knees and walked down the steps. This was the prelude to the Reformation. Was Luther right? Are men justified before God by faith alone? Let us see.

According to the Bible, justification is by faith in Christ; according to Rome, justification is by faith plus works. According to the Bible, justification produces good works; according to Rome, good works produce justification. According to the Bible, justification is by Christ alone; according to Rome, it is by Christ and the sinner. It would appear that the word of Rome and the Word of God are two different things. The following is a formula I have used for over 50 years when explaining this point:

 Roman Catholic Teaching:
Faith + Works → Justification

Biblical Doctrine:
Faith → Justification + Works

It can be seen from the diagram that works are necessary for justification in both systems; but in the Roman system they are necessary as a prerequisite; in the biblical system they are necessary as a postrequisite. (For a much fuller treatment of this entire issue, see the book *Justification by Faith ALONE*, by John MacArthur, R. C. Sproul, John Armstrong, Joel Beeke, and myself, and published by Soli Deo Gloria in 1995.)

But someone will ask, does the Bible not also state that "faith without works is dead" (James 2:20)? Does it not go on to say that such a faith cannot justify? Does it not imply that faith must be supplemented by works in order to avail? Is the Catholic doctrine not right after all: justification is by faith plus works? The answer is simple—justification is by a living and active faith (this is understood everywhere in the Bible; it is made explicit in James). Now, a living faith leads to good works. So justification, which is by a living faith, is by a full-of-the-promise-of-good-works faith. "Justification is by faith alone, but not by the faith that is alone."

Let us endeavor to illustrate what James is teaching here about faith. He is not questioning the ability of genuine faith to justify, but he is simply insisting that it has to be genuine and not "dead" faith. Suppose a man were fortunate enough to have $35 to spend on a hat and went to a store to purchase one. Having selected the one he wished, he hands the salesman his currency only to be told that it is counterfeit and cannot be accepted for payment. Is the dealer saying that the hat cannot be bought for $35? That something more is needed? Is he reflecting on the previously advertised ability of $35 to buy the hat in question? Certainly not. He is only insisting that it be genuine currency. That is all that is necessary, but it *is* necessary. In the same way, James is saying that justification is not by a counterfeit faith. He is not saying that it is not by genuine faith.

"Justification by faith" is really not the precise statement of this doctrine. Justification is by CHRIST ALONE (received by faith). We are not justified by our acceptance of the redeeming mercy of Jesus Christ crucified, but by Christ's mercy (ours by acceptance).

This is the heart of our doctrine—that Christ alone was sufficient for all our sins, that He is able to save to the uttermost those who come to Him in faith. And, conversely, the most serious part of the Roman heresy on this whole doctrine is at this point. By denying justification by faith alone she also denies the sufficiency of Christ's atonement.

We have observed that justification is by faith *in Christ*. Now let us note that justification is by *faith* in Christ. Christ is the ground of justification; faith is the instrument. Christ saves; faith is the means by which Christ's salvation is received. There is no other name than His whereby we must be saved; but there is no other way than by faith. A. H. Strong has likened faith to the coupling which connects a locomotive with its train of cars. It is the locomotive and not the coupling that pulls the train. But without the coupling even the locomotive could not pull the train. It is Christ and not faith that saves the soul. But without faith in Him not even Christ is able to save. (And remember, faith in Christ is the gift of Christ.)

Some fancy that biblical justification is a process rather than an act because it is mentioned at different times in a justified person's life. But its being stated at different times is because different "works" illustrate its continuing activity. It is cited in connection with Abraham's later offering of Isaac, not because he did not possess it earlier, but because that great "work" demonstrated Abraham's faith (which alone justified him, and not that or any

other work). As James said, the work justified (vindi-
cated) the faith (which justified the person).

One concluding word on the fruits of justification.
Rome has always charged that this Protestant doctrine
leads to immorality. Being justified by faith, Rome says,
we have a presumptuous peace with God; we have access
into a grace from which we will constantly fall; and we are
conceitedly assured of heaven and can find no purpose in
tribulation and discipline. But Paul says, "Being justified
by faith, we have peace with God through our Lord Jesus
Christ: by whom also we have access by faith into this
grace wherein we stand, and rejoice in the hope of the
glory of God. And not only so, but we glory in tribulation
also," Romans 5:1–3. Rome, of course, is thinking of a
"counterfeit" grace while the Bible speaks of the genuine
product. History shows that where the doctrine of justification by faith alone has been preached in its purity,
morals have been most rigorous, Christianity most abid-
ing, and good works most abundant. And why should it
not be so, seeing we have been redeemed by the precious
blood of Christ?

Furthermore, "faith without works is dead." No works
—no faith. No faith—no justification. Protestantism has
always been *anti*-antinomian.

And so, when we realize that Jesus has purchased our
redemption by His blood, we say with Paul, 2 Corinthians
5:14–15, "We thus judge that if one died for all then were
all dead . . . that they which live should not henceforth
live unto themselves, but unto Him which died for them
and rose again."

8. CONCLUSION

In a short primer of this kind, it is impossible to deal with the entire Roman system of doctrine. The new Catholic catechism contains over 700 pages of doctrinal teaching of the Catholic church. But perhaps this little primer has helped Protestants and Catholics alike to think through their beliefs. I shall conclude this brief examination of Roman Catholicism by asking three questions:

1. What is the fundamental defect of Roman Catholicism?
2. What are the consequent errors?
3. What should be our attitude towards the Roman Catholic church?

QUESTION 1. What is the fundamental defect of Roman Catholicism?

ANSWER. The fundamental error of Rome is two-fold. It consists in a denial of the authority of God, on the one hand, and a deification of human authority, on the other. Rome rejects the supremacy of God as He has spoken in the Bible. Rather than subject herself to His Word, she subjects His Word to her. Rather than criticize herself in its light, she construes it in her light. On the other hand, she exalts herself to infallibility and would have all men bow down and blindly worship her upon pain of bodily death in the world (if she has the power to enforce it) and spiritual death in the world to come. Not without reason has the Church of Rome been called the greatest tyrant the world has ever seen.

QUESTION 2. What are the consequent errors?

ANSWER. The consequent errors deriving from this original sin of unbounded arrogance are legion. Most im-

portant of all, Rome closes the divine way of salvation. She
has taken Christ from us and we know not where she has
laid Him. All His promises of being the Savior from our
sins, the ransom for our souls, the refuge of our weari-
ness, are gone. The just no longer live by faith. Our freedom is over, we are in bondage again, we are yet in our
sins. In the place of His invitation, her sacraments; in the
place of His mediation, her Virgin, saints, and endless
priests; in the place of Him who was made sin for us that
we might be made the righteousness of God in Him, her
righteousness that leaves us still in our sins. She may
warn, threaten, and excommunicate us, but we reply with
the inspired words of the Apostle Paul, "If any man
preach any other gospel unto you than that ye have received, let him be anathema," Galatians 1:9.

QUESTION 3. But finally, what should be our attitude and policy toward Rome?

May I make a few suggestions? First, our attitude
should be one of humility in judging Rome, not because
of her arrogance but because of our sin. It must be con-
fessed that Protestantism is greatly divided in organiza-
tion, and more divided still in testimony. We have lost the
salt of the Reformation to such a degree that we are almost good for nothing but to be cast out and trodden
under foot of Rome. No longer does the Protestant
church ring with the great themes of salvation by grace,
the authority and genuine inspiration of the Bible, a divine Christ, and a final judgment. We must humbly confess that to a great degree we have been false to our true
gospel and that Rome has been true to her false gospel.
Let us, therefore, set our own house in order.

Second, Protestants should not intermarry with
Romanists. The fact that there are many conscientious

and well-meaning Protestants who have done this and appear to live happily ever afterwards does not make the policy right. The Catholic contract is inimical to Protestantism and cannot be signed by a Protestant without violating evangelical principles. For example, the contract requires the persons to be married by a priest with the understanding that such a marriage alone is valid; it requires the Protestant to promise not to endeavor to win his mate to his faith, which is a violation of his duty as a Christian. Again, it requires the Catholic training of the children, which is detrimental, of course, to the Protestant faith and witness; and it precludes the greatest marital bliss which is based on harmony of religious faith and practice.

Third, Rome should be opposed, but only spiritually. We repudiate the externalistic view of religion and should therefore repudiate all carnal opposition and persecution. Without being either complacent about her, or satisfied with her doctrine, we should nevertheless oppose her kindly. We must fight her, but only with spiritual weapons.

Fourth, we should recognize Roman merits. This series lacks mention of them only because we have been dealing exclusively with fundamentals; on these we feel she errs. We do not mean to suggest that there is not much that is commendable about Rome.

Fifth, we should cooperate wherever possible. In worship it is impossible, in joint moral enterprises it is sometimes possible, and in general social welfare movements it is possible and often imperative.

Sixth, we should bid our Roman Catholic friends to come to the true church. She, in error, invites us. Surely we, in truth, ought to invite her. We bear the Catholics witness that they have a zeal, but not according to knowledge. We pray God that they might all come to an understanding of Christ's all-sufficient sacrifice and be saved.